Jackie Robinson plays baseball with fire in his gut. He can do it all—catch, throw, hit, run. He's so fast, fans call him Comet.

But there is one thing Jackie cannot do: play Major League Baseball. It is 1945. Black players must play in the Negro Leagues.

But one day, Branch Rickey calls Jackie with a plan. Branch runs an all-white team called the Brooklyn Dodgers. He knows that Jackie can help them win.

"I would like you to be on my team," he tells Jackie. "The two of us can end segregation in baseball. But beware. People will try to put a stop to our plan. They will insult you, try to make you angry. Then they will say black players do not belong."

"Are you looking for a black man who is afraid to fight back?" asks Jackie.

"I'm looking for a ballplayer with the guts *not* to fight back," says Branch.

Branch has a point. Jackie agrees to stay silent and become the first black player in the major leagues.

Two years later, Jackie is finally playing for the Dodgers. He grabs his bat and steps to the plate. Fans now call him Destroyer because he blasts baseballs when he swings.

The pitcher throws. The ball buzzes in close. *Thwack!*

It smacks Jackie on the arm. The pitcher glares at Jackie and spits. The fire in Jackie's gut flares up. There is a lot he would like to say. But he cannot. He must let his play do the talking.

Jackie jogs silently to first base. There, his body is coiled like a spring, set to explode. When the pitcher looks back at the catcher, Jackie darts to second base. He's safe!

Brooklyn fans cheer. They like how boldly Jackie plays.

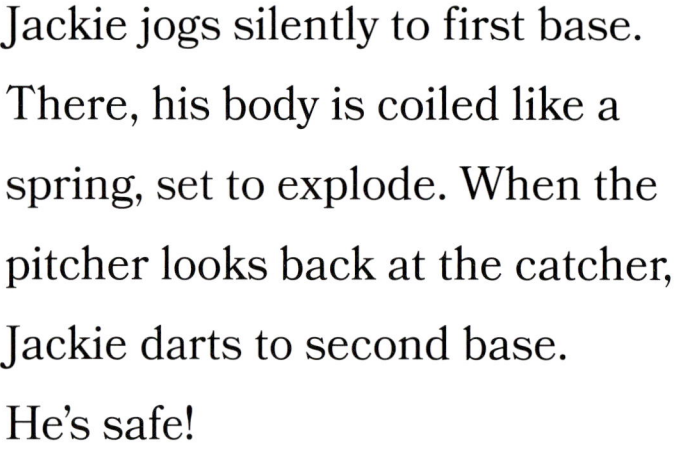

But when the Dodgers play far from home, life is much more difficult for Jackie. Sometimes Jackie must sleep at a different hotel than his teammates. Some places will not let him in to eat. Sometimes he eats on the bus, by himself.

It is the 1940s. Many players and fans do not like to see a black player on a white team. They look at Jackie and jeer.

Still he stays silent.

Jackie tells himself, "One day, I will let the world know what I think."

That day comes four years after Jackie's first call from Branch. For four years, Jackie has stayed silent.

Branch tells him, "You have become a star. Our fans support you. You no longer have to let your play speak for you. You can be yourself now."

Jackie regains his voice. For the rest of his life, he will speak up for justice.